THE GOOD GOLF GUIDE

COURSE STRATEGY

This material previously appeared in *Improve Your Golf*.
This volume compiled by Paul Foston and Sally Hiller.

3298
Published in 1994 by Tiger Books International PLC, London
in association with CLB Publishing, Godalming, Surrey
© Eaglemoss Publications Ltd 1989, 1990, 1991, 1992
All rights reserved
Printed and bound in Hong Kong
ISBN 1-85501-412-2

THE GOOD GOLF GUIDE

COURSE STRATEGY

TIGER BOOKS INTERNATIONAL
LONDON

CONTENTS

1

SET-UP WELL
PAGE 10

2

THE ATHLETIC SWING
PAGE 29

3

TEMPO AND RHYTHM
PAGE 48

4

PREPARATION IS VITAL
PAGE 55

INTRODUCTION

Do you play golf once a fortnight, rarely find the time to practise, and never dream of taking lessons until your game has driven you to the depths of despair? Many golfers fit into this category and it is the reason why they find it so difficult to break 90.

The permutations for a bad shot are so numerous that it is a wonder how a good shot can ever be achieved. But great shots are possible, and with good technique, patience and constant practice, you can become one of that elite group of people who boast a single-figure handicap.

This book takes you back to basics, analysing your aim, grip, stance and posture and moves on to looking in step-by-step detail at various aspects of the swing. Together with tips on preparing for competitions, overcoming nerves and choosing the right teacher, it will help you to get more out of this most challenging of games.

A positive approach Gary Player-style: instead of trying merely to lift the ball out of a greenside bunker he will treat it like any other short game shot and aim to hole it.

SET-UP WELL

Most golfers who miss-hit or strike a shot off line tend to check their swing for the remedy. Quite often, though, it's a case of poor grip, stance, alignment or posture. Your set up is the base on which a repetitive golf swing can be structured. Having mastered the basic set up you need to develop a good pre-shot routine. Remember, one good move leads to another.

Correct set up is vital, with the ball always between two points – opposite your left heel and the centre of your stance. This position varies from driver to short iron.

Aim and grip

Before you can even think about hitting the ball you have to know where you want the ball to go and how to hold the club. Aim and grip are the first two of the fundamentals that must be correct or your shots will be off target. Even the most experienced golfer should constantly check that both his aim and grip are right. It is only too easy for a simple fault to creep into a good golfer's play at the most basic stage.

The concept behind aim applies to whatever type of stroke you are playing. You must have your clubface square to the ball-to-target line to hit the ball straight.

The grip described here is the standard grip – called the overlapping, or Vardon, grip – that you use on every club apart from the putter.

When you've mastered aim and grip you can then go on to think about alignment of your body and club, the ball position in relation to body position, and the posture needed to attain the correct swing. These pre-swing essentials are part of the pre-shot routine that gets you to the right address position – the position from which you can produce a good swing.

AIM THE CLUBFACE

Before you think about the grip, look at the ball and the target – whether it is the flagstick, or some point on the fairway – and imagine a line joining them. This is your ball-to-target line and is the line you want the ball to travel along. Look at your target two or three times to ensure that you see the line clearly in your mind's eye.

You aim the club simply by setting the leading edge of the clubface precisely at right angles to the line from your target to the ball. Rest the sole of the clubhead on the

ground behind the ball, hold the shaft in one hand and set the aim. It doesn't matter too much which club you use but a 6 or 7 iron is a good one to start off with. Stand so that your feet are about as far apart as your shoulders with your toes pointing outwards. The ball is about 1 ft (45cm) from the centre of your toe line.

When you go through the process of adjusting the grip, check every so often that the clubface is square to the ball-to-target line.

GRIP KNOW-HOW

The correct grip is vital and it is easy to adopt. It's important to remember that in the golf swing the hands play different roles and these roles are reflected in the way

ON TARGET
The correct aim and grip are essential if you want to hit the ball accurately and powerfully towards your target. At all times, while assuming the grip, the clubface should be square on to the imaginary line from the ball to the target.

TAKING UP THE OVERLAPPING GRIP

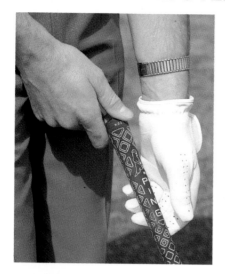

1 BEFORE YOU GRIP
Rest the clubhead on the ground and support the club with your right forefinger and thumb. Let your left arm hang naturally beside the club. Make sure the clubface is properly aimed.

2 THE LEFT HAND
Move your left hand on to the club and position the grip diagonally across the 'meat' of your hand. Close your third and little fingers – vital pressure points.

3 THUMB POSITION
Completely close your left hand, allowing your thumb to rest to the right of centre. Make sure your grip is not too tight.

TAKING AIM

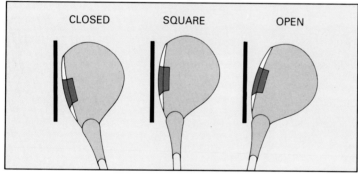

CLOSED   SQUARE   OPEN

The clubhead
Place the clubhead squarely behind the ball. If the clubface is open or closed, the flight of the golf ball is affected. Be extra careful when taking your grip not to alter the angle of the clubface.

they are used in the grip. The hands are placed in different positions and work together during the swing.

Your left hand supports the club and maintains the clubhead in the correct position through impact with the ball. It can be described as the 'strong hand' in the grip. The club is positioned diagonally across the palm, resting against the 'meat' of your hand.

Your right hand, however, is going to 'release' the club-head just before impact. This release gives the clubhead the power and speed to get maximum distance.

Releasing the clubhead is similar to the action of throwing a golf ball or skimming stones across water. When you do this you instinctively hold the stone somewhere between the forefinger and middle finger, with the thumb resting lightly on it as a support.

The release comes from the 'trig-ger finger' or, to be more precise, the middle joint of your forefinger.

When you hold the club with your right hand the grip should run through these fingers. By holding it this way you can be sure of a good release of power at the cor-rect time.

When taking your grip, start by placing the sole of the club on the

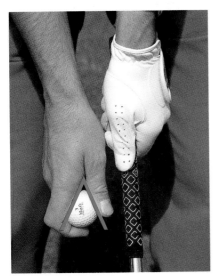

4 FORMING THE 'V'
Create the 'V', between thumb and forefinger, by holding a golf ball between the forefinger, middle finger and thumb of your right hand. Drop the ball by slightly releasing the pressure but keep your hand in the same position.

pro tip

Not so tight a squeeze

There's a simple way to get your grip pressure correct. Take a large tube of toothpaste and unscrew the cap. Hold the tube with the nozzle pointing down and grip the tube as you would your club. The pressure you exert should be just hard enough to hold the tube securely without squeezing the toothpaste out.

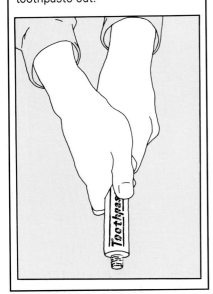

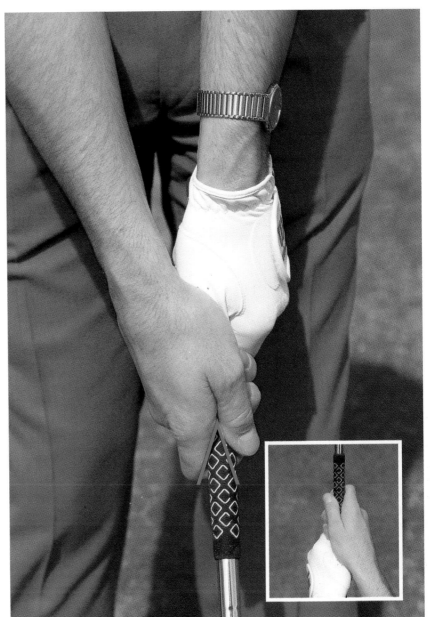

5 THE RIGHT HAND
Move your right hand on to the grip and hold the club with your two middle fingers and forefinger. Let your little finger overlap with the forefinger of your left hand and your right thumb rest to the left of centre of the shaft. Raise the club up to eye level. You should see two knuckles showing on each hand and a 'V' made by the thumb and forefinger of your right hand.

ground – preferably up against the ball on a tee peg as this helps you keep the clubhead square. Support the club using the tip of your right forefinger and thumb placed on the top of the grip.

THE LEFT HAND

Let your left arm hang naturally by the side of the grip before bringing it across to the club to take hold. About -1in (1.5-2.5cm) of the grip protrudes above where it rests across your hand. Your thumb should fall slightly to the right of centre and your third and little fingers should grip hardest. These are important pressure points. The club must rest diagonally across your palm, in the 'meat' of your hand.

THE RIGHT HAND

When you have the club correctly positioned in your left hand let go with your right hand and let it hang naturally by your side. The grip formed by your right hand should take up the form of a 'V' between your thumb and forefinger.

To get an idea of how the 'V' should look, hold a golf ball as if you are about to throw it. Drop the ball by slightly relaxing your grip and, with the grip still in place, bring your hand across to the club.

Grip the club below your left hand with the middle two fingers and forefinger of your right hand. Let the little finger of your right hand overlap with the forefinger of your left hand. The thumb of your right hand should rest lightly on the grip pointing down the shaft and slightly to the left of centre. Check that the clubface is square.

When you have both hands on the club, lift it up to chest height. Take a good look at your hands – you should see two knuckles on each of your hands and a very pronounced 'V' in your right hand, pointing towards your chin. The hands are now completely moulded into one unit.

OVERLAPPING GRIP
In the finished grip, the little finger of your right hand is over the forefinger of your left hand. It is the standard grip (also called Vardon grip) for all shots except putts. It is the best grip for most golfers.

INTERLOCKING GRIP
If you have small hands or fingers try the interlocking grip. This is the same as the overlapping grip except that the little finger of your right hand interlocks with the forefinger of your left hand.

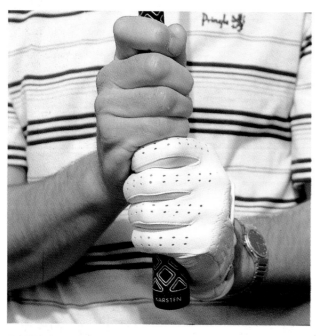

BASEBALL GRIP
This is an unusual grip in which all ten fingers are in contact with the grip. It is mainly used by players who are physically weak, such as youngsters and those suffering from arthritis.

pro tip

Leave a space
When taking your grip leave -1in (1.5-2.5cm) of the grip showing above your left hand. This secures your hold and prevents you straining the back two tendons of the left hand. It also prevents overswinging.

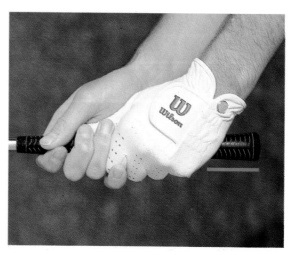

Posture and alignment

The right posture sets up your body in the correct position for the swing and proper alignment ensures that you hit the ball straight along the imaginary ball-to-target line.

Body position and alignment of the body are two of the five essentials necessary for a good swing, along with aim of the clubface, grip and ball placement. You need to know these basics and practise them regularly until you don't have to think about them before you make your swing.

POSTURE

Correct posture is vital. Just watch the top players on TV. Although the world's great golfers may swing the club differently, they all have identical posture at address when they are preparing to strike the ball.

Before you take up your posture, hold your club in your right hand and place the clubhead behind the ball, check that you are aiming the clubhead correctly and take your grip on the club. Use a 6, 7 or 8 iron as these three clubs are all easy to swing.

There are three stages on the path to correct posture. The first is your stance – where you place your feet when you address the ball. The two other stages involve your knees and back.

POSTURE AT ADDRESS
Flex your knees and stick your bottom out slightly. Your hands should lie directly below your chin. The angle of your back allows your shoulders to rotate easily. Keep your chin up so it is clear of your left shoulder during the backswing.

FROM THE FRONT
Your left arm, your hands and the clubhead can be joined by an imaginary straight line. The ball is in the centre of your stance and your hands are slightly ahead of the ball.

THE RIGHT STANCE

Your feet should be as far apart as your shoulders are wide. In other words you take up a shoulder-width stance. They should also be at a slight outwards angle. The best way to get your feet at the correct angle is to imagine you are standing on the centre of a big clockface. Your right foot should point to 1 o'clock and your left to 11 o'clock.

Once your feet are in the right place, lift the club off the ground, and stand upright and at ease, with your legs straight. Now go on to the next stage.

Keeping your legs straight, bend your torso so that you are leaning forwards with your weight on the balls of your feet.

Finally, bend your knees slightly and let your bottom stick out. This should straighten your back. A straight back at the correct angle to the vertical allows your body to rotate properly when you make your swing.

This final stage also moves your body weight back from the balls of your feet to a more central position. You should always be comfortable and balanced when you have correct posture.

ALIGNMENT

Correct alignment means lining up your body parallel to the ball-to-target line. This may sound easy, but very few golfers achieve it or realize its importance in making sure the ball goes straight and accurately to the target.

Too many golfers take up what they feel is the ideal grip and posture without understanding the correct alignment procedure. Preparation for a shot is as vital as making the stroke itself.

BALL-TO-TARGET LINE

Before aligning yourself for a shot, you must first re-check your aim so that your clubface is square on

Hands below your chin
To check your hand position, try tying a small weight to the end of a piece of string, about 2ft (60cm) long. Grip the other end between your teeth and let the weight hang freely. The string should pass along the same line as your grip.

THE CORRECT POSTURE

1 POSITION OF FEET
Your feet at address must be the same width apart as your shoulders. They should also point slightly outwards.

2 LEAN FORWARD
Stand at ease with your legs straight then lean forward so that your weight is on the balls of your feet. Place the clubhead squarely behind the ball.

TRAINING ALIGNMENT

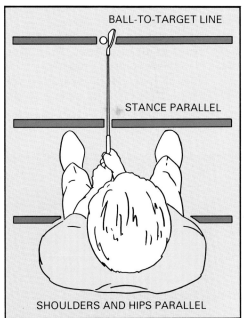

ALIGN YOUR BODY
Alignment can be surprisingly hard to get right. Your shoulders, especially, must not point at the target but must be parallel to the ball-to-target line.

ON TRACK
One tried and tested way to achieve perfect alignment is to imagine a railway track between your ball and the target. The ball and clubhead are on the far rail, which runs to the base of the target, while the tips of your toes touch the nearside rail. Align your shoulders, hips and knees so that they are parallel to this nearside rail.

3 BEND YOUR KNEES
Bend your knees and stick your bottom out slightly. This straightens your back. Add the correct grip. The club should rest firmly on the ground.

RAILWAY FORMATION
You can make the imaginary railway line idea clearer by placing a number of clubs on the ground in railway line formation. Line up your clubface square on to the club furthest away from you, while taking a stance parallel to the near line. Although your feet and body point left of target, they are in fact correctly placed: parallel to the ball-to-target line.

to the ball-to-target line. It's essential to remember that your body must be parallel to this line. To help do this, imagine another line running between the tips of your big toes.

This line should run parallel to the ball-to-target line. Your knees, hips and shoulders must also be parallel to this new line running from toe to toe.

It might feel as if your shoulders are aiming left of the target but remember you strike the ball with the clubface. Aligning your shoulders *parallel* to the ball-to-target line is vital for creating the perfect swing.

Aligning your shoulders so they point *at* the target is a common fault which makes the club aim too far right. It often occurs when a golfer lines up a shot by looking at the target over the left shoulder. Avoid it by rotating – rather than lifting – your head to check that your clubface is aimed properly. Check your aim several times before you play a stroke that is square to the ball-to-target line.

PRACTISING AIM AND ALIGNMENT

1 VIEW FROM BEHIND
First, view the shot from behind – it's easier to find the intended line of flight. Pick out a marker such as a divot 3ft (1m) beyond the ball on the target line.

2 AIM THE CLUBFACE
Holding the club in your right hand, place the clubhead on the ground behind the ball and aim it square on to the selected marker.

3 TAKE A PARALLEL STANCE
Take a stance parallel to the ball-to-marker line, and grip the club correctly using both hands. Keep the ball central in your stance.

Practise this routine regularly until it becomes as natural as walking. Remember, you must always find the correct alignment before you consider playing the shot.

Ball position and the swing

The last of the five pre-swing essentials to know before learning about the swing is where you place the ball in relation to your feet when you are using the various clubs.

In the normal golf swing, the clubface must be square on to the ball-to-target line at impact. Knowing what goes on during the swing and what happens to the clubface during the swing helps you to get your clubface square on to the ball-to-target line at impact.

CLUB AND STANCE

Depending on the type of club, you stand with your feet further or closer apart. Once you've decided how far apart your feet should be you can then go on and accurately position your ball.

The longer the shaft of your club, the wider apart you have your feet. So your stance is wider for the longer irons such as a 2 or 3 iron and a driver and is narrower for the shorter clubs such as the 8 or 9 irons and the wedges. With a 2 iron,

for instance, your stance should be about as wide as a normal walking pace is long. With a short iron such as a sand wedge you stand with your feet about half as far apart as for a long iron. With a 6 or 7 iron your feet are about shoulder width apart.

PLACING THE BALL

The general rule is: the shorter the shaft, the more central the ball

should be in your stance. If you are using a 9 iron, position the ball in the centre of your stance. With a 2 iron, place the ball opposite the inside of your left heel.

For the clubs in between, place the ball between these two positions. When using a medium iron, for instance, place the ball midway between the centre of your stance and the inside of your left heel.

The length of each club's shaft

PLACEMENT AND STANCE
Correct placement is determined by the club you are using. With a medium iron such as a 7 iron, the ball should be placed on a line midway between the inside of your left heel and the centre of your stance. The width of a 7-iron stance is just over half the length of a normal walking stride.

also determines how far away from the ball that you stand. For a long-shafted club such as a 2 iron the ball is further away from you than for a shorter-shafted, high-numbered club.

POSTURE AND SWING PLANE

The ball is placed in these different positions because of the changes to posture brought about by the length of the differing clubs. The shorter the shaft, the nearer you are to the ball, the narrower your stance and the more your back is bent.

It is the angle of your back at address that influences swing plane. The more bent it is the steeper your swing plane. With a longer-shafted club, such as a 2 iron, the ball is further from your feet than with a 9

iron. Your hands are higher and your back is more upright. This automatically creates a flatter swing plane around your body.

The shape of your swing affects the angle at which the clubhead hits the ball, and dictates the amount and type of spin. The steep swing plane of the 9 iron creates backspin, while the flatter plane of the 2 iron produces overspin. Backspin prevents the ball running as far as normal on landing, while overspin increases roll.

SWING PATH

During a correct swing the clubhead travels in a path from the inside of the ball-to-target line, briefly along the ball-to-target line at impact and then back inside the ball-to-target line after impact. It

THE SWING

1 TAKEAWAY
In the first 6-9in (15-23cm) of the backswing, the club moves in a straight line. It has yet to be influenced by your upper body.

CLUBS, POSTURE AND PLACEMENT

● BALL OPPOSITE
INSIDE LEFT HEEL

● BALL MID-WAY
BETWEEN LEFT
HEEL AND CENTRE
OF STANCE

● BALL IN CENTRE
OF STANCE

3 IRON (LONG IRON)
Your back is slightly bent at address and the width of your stance is equal to the length of a normal walking stride. Place the ball opposite the inside of your left heel.

7 IRON (MEDIUM IRON)
The shaft is shorter so your feet are closer together and your back is more bent. The ball is placed closer to your feet and positioned midway between the centre of your stance and opposite your inside left heel.

SAND WEDGE (SHORT IRON)
At address, your back is more bent than it is with either a long or medium iron. The ball is closer to your feet and is placed in the centre of your stance.

2 NATURAL ROTATION
By the mid-point of the backswing the body rotation moves the club inside the ball-to-target line. This also opens the clubface.

3 THE HIGHEST POINT
Near the top of the backswing, the club continues its path around the body. At the top, the shaft of the club should be parallel with the target.

4 DOWNSWING
The downswing is almost identical to the backswing. The club follows a path inside the ball-to-target line and the clubface closes.

5 SQUARE CONTACT
The clubface gradually returns, from being open at the start of the downswing, to being perfectly square to the ball-to-target line at impact. The club travels briefly along the ball-to-target line at impact.

6 THROUGHSWING
On the throughswing, the club continues along its path and moves back inside the ball-to-target line. The clubface continues to rotate and gradually closes as the throughswing continues.

never goes outside the ball-to-target line.

At the start of the backswing, turning your body moves the clubhead inside the ball-to-target line. It also causes the clubface to open and, at the mid-point of the backswing, its face has opened so that it is at an angle of 90° to the ball-to-target line.

CLUBFACE AT IMPACT

During the downswing and right up to impact the clubhead gradually closes and only at one brief moment – impact – is the clubface square to the ball-to-target line. On the throughswing the face continues to rotate and closes.

SWING PLANES

A perfect in-to-in swing path alone does not guarantee square contact. The ball must also be correctly placed in relation to your stance. Golf is often said to be a game of inches. One inch off target on the tee can mean 10-15 yards off line down the fairway.

When the ball is too far back in the stance, the club meets it too early on the downswing. The clubface is still open and, even with the correct in-to-in swing path, the ball goes to the right of target.

If the ball is too far forward in the stance, the club makes contact too late (on the throughswing). The clubface has closed slightly and the ball lands left of target.

It's easier to place the ball correctly once you understand each club's swing plane. The swing plane for a 3 iron (pink) is flatter than that of a shorter 7 iron (green). Your spine is more upright and produces a sweeping action around your body, with the clubhead reaching its lowest point at a later stage in the swing path. The ball is therefore placed further forward in the stance than for the 7 iron.

3 IRON

7 IRON

Toeing the line
To help understand the opening and closing of the clubface during the swing path, slowly swing club back and through the normal swing plane. At the mid-point on both the backswing and the throughswing, the toe of the club should point directly at the sky. At these points, the face should also be open by 90° and closed by 90° respectively.

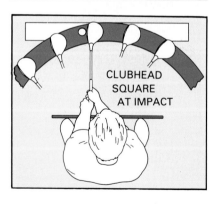

IN-TO-IN CLUBHEAD
During the correct in-to-in swing path, the clubhead should never move outside the ball-to-target line. Note how the clubface is square to the target at one point only – impact.

Pre-shot routine

Learn and use a good pre-shot routine to eliminate the faults that can occur before you make any strike. Correct preparation helps you to become more consistent, which in turn lowers your score.

The pre-shot routine is a blend of mental and physical stages that leads you to the right position and frame of mind to hit the ball where you want it to go. You should build a consistent pre-shot routine into your game at an early stage.

The physical aspects of it – where you achieve the correct address position through a series of actions – are usually quite easy to pick up and perform.

The mental aspects – visualizing where you want the ball to go and then deciding on the type of stroke you want to play – can be a bit hard at first. But visualizing does improve with experience and in the long run is the key to lower scores.

The visualizing aspect of your pre-shot routine begins the moment you walk on to the tee, or

ASSESSING THE SHOT

Pre-shot routine starts as you approach the ball or teeing off area and assess the factors involved in making the shot.

DISTANCE
Try to judge the distance between your ball and the target – use a distance chart if there is one.

HAZARDS
Make a mental note of the hazards that lie between your ball and the target, such as the bunker and rough here. Check the position of the pin, and look for any slopes.

WEATHER AND COURSE CONDITIONS
Find out the direction and strength of the wind – if there is any – and assess the condition of both the fairway and green. Are they damp, dry or even bone hard? The state of the ground affects the amount of roll on the ball.

CHOOSE YOUR CLUB
Choose the best club for the stroke from your knowledge of distance, hazards, and the probable effect of weather and course conditions.

SHAPE THE SHOT
Decide on the best line to the target. Is it right, left, or centre? Your choice of club might affect the decision. A high shot can clear hazards, while a low running shot doesn't. Visualize the ball's path.

FEEL THE SWING
Picture and feel the stroke in your mind before making a few practice swings.

PREPARING TO HIT

1 STAND BEHIND THE BALL
Stand behind the ball and select your ball-to-target line. Pick a small mark (such as a divot hole, leaf or twig) on that line, no more than a club's length from your ball.

2 AIM THE CLUBFACE
Hold the club in your right hand and place the clubhead behind the ball. Aim the clubface square on to the ball-to-mark-to-target line.

when you reach your ball on the fairway.

PREPARING TO VISUALIZE

Visualizing is a two-part process: assessing the difficulty of the shot by studying the hazards and course conditions, and deciding on the type of stroke you want to play so that you can set about shaping the shot in your mind.

If you are new to golf, you may find it difficult to visualize. Although assessment of hazards and course conditions is quite easy to grasp, deciding on the shape of your shot takes a little longer to perfect.

ASSESS THE PROBLEMS

You have to assess a number of factors. You can't just walk up to the ball, take a swipe at it and hope it goes the correct distance and in the right direction.

First, judge the distance your ball is from the target – whether this is a flag on the green or a

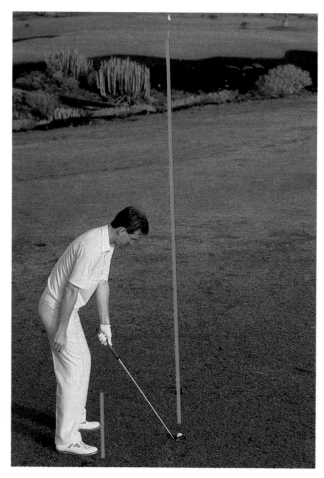

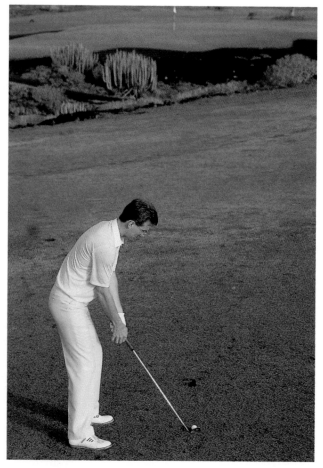

3 TAKE A PARALLEL STANCE
Align your feet and body parallel to the ball-to-mark-to-target line, and adopt the ideal posture. Take the correct grip with your left hand.

4 COMPLETE THE GRIP
Add your right hand to the club to complete the grip. Check that the clubface is still aimed square on to the ball-to-mark-to-target line.

position on the fairway. Make a mental note of the hazards that come into play, such as out-of-bounds posts, ditches, trees, bunkers and streams. Also note exactly where the pin is and any fairway slopes.

Second, assess weather and course conditions as these dictate which club you should use. Check for wind, its direction and strength. Is the fairway or green damp or dry and how is the ball likely to run? Even when playing from familiar tees and fairways, you need to re-assess club selection because of changing conditions.

When you have analysed hazards and conditions, select your club.

SHAPING THE SHOT

Now decide on the type of shot you want to play, and imagine the intended flight path of the ball. To visualize the path of the ball, you must shape the shot. For example, if all the trouble is on the right side of the fairway, it is best to play down the left. If the fairway is narrow, you might want to use an iron, not a wood, from the tee for accuracy.

Visualize the ball travelling through the air, landing on the green or fairway, and rolling towards the target.

The key to shaping your shot is knowing your capabilities. You must know the distance you can hit with each club and understand the flight path of the ball in each shot. The average player hits a wedge shot between 100 and 110yd (90 and 100m), with a 10yd (9m) difference between each successive club.

As your swing develops and your timing improves, your game becomes more consistent and it is easier to judge the distance you achieve with each club. Your swing must be repeatable. Inconsistency creeps in if your tempo varies from shot to shot.

Your tempo has to remain the same before you can develop a feel for distance. Only when you know

the level of your own ability can you attempt to shape the shot.

Once you have shaped your shot, 'feel' the swing in your mind before removing the chosen club from your bag. Then take a couple of practice swings.

Learning to visualize your shots takes experience, so don't worry if

Don't be rushed
Never rush your pre-shot routine. Hurrying your preparation leads to a quick, jerky stroke. Stay relaxed and calm at all times. Then you can maintain a smooth rhythm and tempo from the moment you start visualizing your shot, through to pre-shot routine and to making the stroke itself. Be deliberate and remember there is no time limit for playing a shot. If you feel tension creeping into your grip, lift the club off the ground and jiggle it.

5 REMOVE TENSION
Lift the club off the ground and waggle it in your hands. Move your feet at the same time to release tension. Check your aim by looking at the target.

6 FINAL ADDRESS POSITION
The pre-shot routine is now complete and you're in a position to play the shot. Careful preparation is the key to a correct swing and successful shot.

on the first few occasions it is very much a case of trial and error.

PREPARING TO HIT

Having selected your club and decided on the type of shot you want to play, you now have to adopt the correct address position by following a number of stages.

This routine builds up the correct grip, posture and alignment and puts you in a relaxed and confident frame of mind. It gives you the best possible chance of making a good stroke. As with the visualizing stages of the pre-shot routine, you must go through these physical stages every time you play a shot, whether on tee or fairway.

BALL-TO-TARGET LINE

Stand behind the ball and select your intended ball-to-target line. Choose a small mark, such as a twig, leaf or divot hole, about a club's length in front of the ball and on that same ball-to-target line.

Hold the club in your right hand, and place the sole of the clubhead behind the ball, aiming the club-face square on to the mark. Then stand parallel to the ball-to-marker line and adopt the correct posture. Your knees, hips and shoulders must also be parallel to this line. Add the correct grip, before checking that the clubface is still aimed properly.

Rid yourself of any tension by lifting the club off the ground and waggling it in your hands. Move your feet up and down in sympathy. This relaxes your body and muscles, and allows you to swing freely and correctly. Tension creeps in at address when the body becomes rigid. You have to remove it before you make any stroke.

A consistent pre-shot routine is as important as the swing itself.

How much wind?
To detect the amount of wind, throw a few blades of grass into the air above your head and see where and how fast they are blown. You may need to repeat this action to confirm wind strength and direction. Club selection varies considerably in windy conditions.

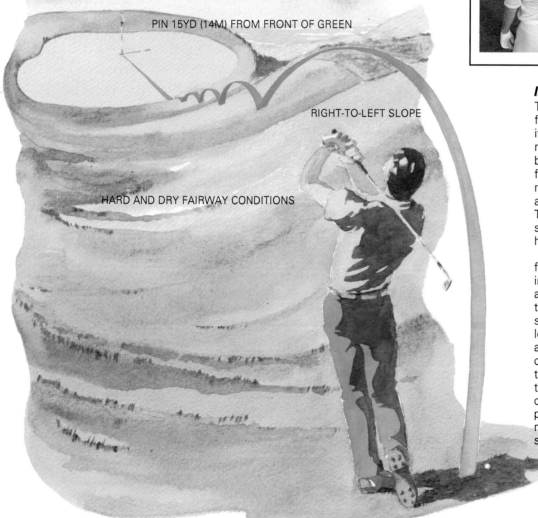

PIN 15YD (14M) FROM FRONT OF GREEN

RIGHT-TO-LEFT SLOPE

HARD AND DRY FAIRWAY CONDITIONS

BALL 160YD (146M) FROM PIN

Imagine the ball's path
Try to imagine the ball's flight, where you expect it to land and how it might run. This golfer's ball is 160yd (146m) from the flag, there are no hazards, but there is a right-to-left slope. There is no wind and the surface of the fairway is hard and dry.

He chooses a 7 iron for the shot, as he intends to land the ball about 20yd (18m) from the green. Because the slope is from right to left, he aims his shot about 15yd (14m) right of the pin. The slope will then carry his ball towards the flag. He completes his final practice swing and is now ready to make the stroke.

Curing tension with Nicklaus

Mental tension on the golf course leads to physical tension – and tense muscles mean that you feel clumsy and awkward and your score suffers.

Tension at address can be avoided if you learn a simple pre-shot routine which keeps all parts of your body relaxed, on the move and ready to go. Then you can start your swing smoothly and comfortably by keeping your body moving as you prepare for the shot.

Jack Nicklaus, one of the greatest golfers, has built such a system into his game. He is famous for his precise and methodical approach to every shot. Nicklaus' pre-shot routine has helped him to stay that little bit cooler than his rivals under pressure.

THE TWO C'S

As he stands on the tee, Nicklaus remembers two c's: confidence

NICKLAUS' PRE-SWING
The way to cure mental and physical tension as you stand to the ball is to develop a repeatable pre-shot routine for every stroke. Jack Nicklaus stays absorbed by going through the same movements every time and keeping all the important parts of his body moving.

Soft forearms mean a relaxed grip. Slightly firming up his grip, while making sure it stays soft, is Jack's swing trigger.

The waggle reduces tension because it keeps your body moving. It also boosts muscle memory and helps you to see the shot.

Alternatively moving your feet lightly up and down relaxes your legs.
This helps to keep you mobile and ready to swing smoothly.

and concentration.

Confidence comes from being able to repeat successful shots in tough situations – and for that you need experience and practice.

Use self-discipline to make yourself concentrate by going through the same movements before you play each shot.

REPEAT YOUR ROUTINE

Always run through your pre-shot checkpoints: set-up, correct

INTERLOCKING GRIP

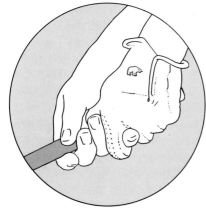

Jack uses the interlocking grip, which is helpful if you have small hands. It is rare among the top players, who use the standard grip.

club-face aim and body alignment. Jack always checks aim by selecting a marker (a leaf or patch of grass) a few paces in front of his ball directly along the ball-to-target line.

Aim and alignment take time. Jack releases tension by keeping his body moving all the time in the address position. His feet move lightly up and down, in time with gentle swinging back and forth of the club.

This swinging of the club – known as the 'waggle' – serves as the preparation for the shot. Nicklaus waggles the club along the line he intends to start the backswing. His waggle is different for every shot: it varies for a fade, a draw or a conventional straight shot.

STAY SOFT

Tension before starting your backswing leads to one particular path of destruction – gripping too tightly. It's impossible to swing smoothly with too firm a grip – it causes a jerky takeaway.

As you stand at address, check that your forearms are 'soft' – if your forearms feel supple, you have the correct relaxed grip pressure. Rigid forearms always mean your grip is too tight.

All that remains in this simple, repeatable procedure is to trigger the swing. Jack uses the 'stationary press' – firming up his grip by pressing his hands together a couple of times and relaxing them. It puts his muscles on 'action stations', without making them tense. Copy it to give you an effective ignition for a smooth swing.

Clubhead off the ground
Jack Nicklaus does not ground the club at address. He says the habit started at Scioto, the club where he learnt to play. The ball used to sit up in the fescue grass rough on the course, and grounding the club sometimes made the ball roll. Young Jack was always concerned about collecting a stroke penalty for moving the ball – so he started to hold the club off the ground.

It has other advantages, too. First, lifting the clubhead and waggling it lessens tension. Second, nothing can impede a smooth takeaway. Third, there is no danger of rule-breaking by grounding the club in a bunker.

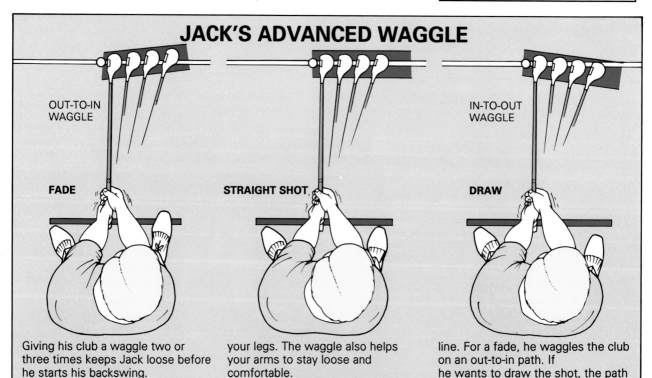

JACK'S ADVANCED WAGGLE

OUT-TO-IN WAGGLE

IN-TO-OUT WAGGLE

FADE

STRAIGHT SHOT

DRAW

Giving his club a waggle two or three times keeps Jack loose before he starts his backswing.

To waggle effectively, include the 'moving parts' of your body that you use in the backswing. Moving your feet lightly up and down sends a feeling of mobility to

your legs. The waggle also helps your arms to stay loose and comfortable.

Nicklaus is always careful to waggle along the line he wants to start the backswing. On a normal straight shot, he waggles back and through along the ball-to-target

line. For a fade, he waggles the club on an out-to-in path. If he wants to draw the shot, the path of the waggle is in to out.

This process enhances his confidence, muscle memory and visualization.

2

THE ATHLETIC SWING

Many players rely too much on their hands and arms to hit the ball. Generally there is insufficient body rotation in both directions, which makes consistency difficult. Whilst it is true to say that a person's flexibility will govern the level of movement attained, with specific golfing exercises you can develop a more athletic swing.

Ian Woosnam displays his power play during the 1986 Open at Turnberry.

Swing with your body

A complete body action brings together the relevant parts of the golf swing to give you greater consistency. Your shoulders, arms and body move in one piece to help you groove a repeatable swing into your game.

When different parts of your body move independently there's a risk of faults creeping in. A loose, wristy action may give you the occasional good result in a relaxed game. But without precision timing you're bound to lack consistency. A loose swing can desert you completely when the pressure is on.

Nick Faldo is the greatest exponent of the swing with the body. Next time you have a chance to watch him – perhaps when a tournament is televised – notice how

ENHANCE CONTROL
Playing within yourself is one of the keys to consistent golf – most poor shots result from trying to do too much. The swing with your body builds in control. A towel under the arms keeps the swing compact and prevents you from overswinging or trying to hit the ball too hard. With the towel in place, shoot practice balls to a precise spot about 140yd (128m) away.

SWING WITH BODY PRACTICE DRILL

1 NORMAL AT ADDRESS
Hit shots with a towel held securely under your arms to help you swing with the body – your objective is to keep the towel in place throughout. Adopt your normal address position using no more than a 7 iron.

2 SLOWLY BACK
Swing smoothly away from the ball keeping your arms close to your body. Let the left arm dominate to encourage a full shoulder turn. Keep the right elbow close to your side to stop the arms moving on an upright plane.

3 THREE-QUARTER BACKSWING

Stop the backswing well short of horizontal – remember the emphasis is on control and accuracy. Make sure you complete a full shoulder turn to place the club on the correct plane. The body is nicely coiled behind the ball.

4 WEIGHT SHIFT

Start transferring your weight on to the left side as you begin the downswing. Keep your arms close to your body to lead the clubhead down to the ball from inside the line. This arm action also prevents the towel from slipping.

FOLLOWTHROUGH PRACTICE

5 HANDS RELEASE
The left side provides support as the clubhead travels from in to in through impact. The hands release and your arms pull your body round to face the target – the movement through the ball is effortless.

6 COMPACT FOLLOWTHROUGH
The followthrough position is compact and tidy, with perfect control from start to finish. Vary your practice routine to gain maximum benefit – hit five shots holding the towel in place and five without the towel.

ARMS AND UPPER BODY MOVE TOGETHER

pro tip

Belt help

Improvise with the belt from your trousers to help you groove your swing on the practice ground. You need the help of a friend to fasten the belt correctly – it should fit snugly round your upper arms just above the elbow at address.

Turn your shoulder as you do on a full shot and notice how your arms are held close to the body. This is one of the fundamentals of the swing with your body – it encourages you to swing on a flatter plane for consistency.

HARNESS YOUR SWING
A strap designed by the famous teaching professional David Leadbetter is an effective aid to help you swing with the body.

The strap links your arms and upper body at address and keeps them connected throughout the swing. With regular practice you gradually build the correct moves into your swing.

The strap is on sale in some pro shops. According to the rules of golf it's an artificial aid – you can use it only in practice and never in a competitive round.

rhythmical and compact the swing is, and how fluent his action – no single part of the body moves out of time with another.

Remember, control is the essence of a swing with your body. Never sacrifice accuracy to strive for distance – always swing the club at a tempo that allows you to feel in charge of the clubhead throughout the stroke. Think minimum effort and maximum control.

ONE PIECE TAKEAWAY

The first part of the swing is with your shoulders, arms and club moving smoothly as one away from the ball. Everything moves together to increase your chances of starting the swing on the correct plane.

The coiling of your upper body naturally pulls the left knee in towards the ball – this allows your hips to turn along with the rest of

your body. Your backswing should feel compact but not tense – your right elbow remains close to your side.

If you pick the club up too quickly on the backswing and don't turn properly, the clubhead is thrown in all directions. This excessive wrist movement involves a great deal of guess work – you trust luck more than judgement to place the club in the correct position.

FULL SHOULDER TURN

A one piece takeaway helps you to swing the club on a wide arc and so achieve a full shoulder turn. These moves place the club on the correct plane at the top of your backswing.

A good swing with your body pulls you into a coiled position behind the ball. Your weight is supported on the right side and your upper back faces the target at the top of the backswing.

If you don't turn properly on the backswing all sorts of problems arise. Your swing plane becomes very upright and easily drifts towards an out-to-in path. You suffer the frustration of cutting across the ball and lose distance on your shots.

It's important to maintain control of the clubhead at the top of the backswing – you don't want to ruin the good work achieved earlier in the swing by making a poor downswing.

SMOOTHLY DOWN

The movement down towards the ball is in one piece, with your shoulders, arms and lower body working in harmony. Shift your weight smoothly to the left.

As the body unwinds on the downswing your hands release the clubhead through impact with tremendous speed. The wide arc of your swing generates the power – no longer should you feel the need for a huge lunge at the ball, which upsets your rhythm and timing.

Almost immediately your striking of the ball benefits from an improvement in consistency. Your poor shots are less wild and far less frequent.

✗ FLYING ELBOW
If a towel falls from under your right elbow before you complete the backswing, look carefully at the movement of your arms away from the ball.

A flying right elbow is caused by picking the club up too quickly and moving outside the line on the backswing. Your swing then lacks the necessary width and power – this fault usually results in a sliced shot.

✓ KEEP IT COMPACT
Swing the club smoothly away from the ball, moving your arms and upper body in one piece – concentrate on making a full shoulder turn.

Your right arm folds during the backswing and the elbow points straight down. This solid, compact position puts you on the correct plane at the top of the backswing.

ONE PIECE PUTT
Improve your putting stroke by practising a shorter version of the swing with your body. Place a club under your arms and adopt your normal putting stance.

Swing the putter smoothly back and through keeping the wrists firm. The triangle shape formed by your arms and shoulders should remain constant. The club under your arms points parallel to the ball-to-target line throughout the stroke.

Swing checklist
● Remember, a good backswing places the club on the correct plane at the top and makes it easier to swing down towards the ball correctly. Think of your arms and the club swinging together away from the ball – if you keep the parts moving in one piece you can concentrate on one thought alone.

● The practice ground is the best place to attempt the swing with your body, so make constructive use of your time there. Swing smoothly and always work on your rhythm. If you swing quickly there's very little time to think what you're doing and it's hard to identify faults.

● When you practise the swing with your body try to stay relaxed, both at address and during the swing. Often when you introduce new moves into your game the tendency is to tense up. But a rigid swing prevents you gaining benefit from the change.

Improve your backswing

A strong backswing makes a great difference to a player's game. The aim is to get the clubhead and your hands, arms and body positioned so that you easily and powerfully return the clubface square to the ball.

It's vital to set up the backswing properly – errors at this first stage of the swing are difficult to put right later on.

Before you make a swing, check the basics. Make sure that grip and ball position are correct. With a relaxed posture, align your feet, knees, hips, chest and shoulders parallel to the ball-to-target line.

Although the swing plane and swing path differ from club to club, the technique remains the same. Your posture varies depending on the length of the shaft, but in all cases your knees must be flexed and your back slightly bent. If your back is either too upright or too hunched, or your legs are locked

THE TOP POINT
At the top of the backswing the clubface must be positioned so you can easily return it square to the ball. To achieve this, from address your upper body rotates halfway – about 90° – and your hips, thighs and knees make a quarter turn of 45°. With a full swing, using a wood or long iron, the shaft of the club points at the target – and is parallel to the ball-to-target line.

PERFECT YOUR BACKSWING

1 BE RELAXED
At address you should feel relaxed. Your posture must be correct for your body to rotate fully. Your knees are flexed and your back is slightly bent. Your feet should be about the same distance apart as your shoulders.

2 KEEP CLUBHEAD LOW
With your hands and arms, take the clubhead away, keeping it low to the ground for the first 1ft (30cm). From here allow your body to rotate to the right. This moves the clubhead inside the ball-to-target line. The clubhead feels closed.

straight, it is impossible to make a full body turn.

Get these basics right and you should make a perfect backswing.

SMOOTH AND SLOW TAKEAWAY

It's vital that you set the right tone for the swing by staying smooth and relaxed

The backswing starts with a unified takeaway, as your hands, arms, shoulders, chest and hips move together.

For the first 1ft (30cm) the clubhead stays close to the ground. From here, the backswing is shaped by your left side – the left shoulder and hip start to rotate to the right (vice versa if you're left handed). This pulls your arms and hands in the same direction and the clubhead moves back and inside the ball-to-target line.

Your left knee moves to the right to allow your hips and shoulders to rotate further. Let your upper body move as one.

From an even distribution at address, your weight then moves on to the inside of your right foot.

MID POINT

Your body continues to rotate to the left and by the mid point on the backswing your right arm starts to fold.

Let your left arm remain comfortably straight but not locked. If you've rotated correctly, by the mid point your left hand, left wrist, left arm and left shoulder should be

joined by an imaginary straight line.

As you rotate further your weight continues to move on to your right side and your right hip feels most of the pressure. But don't let your weight transfer to the outside of your right foot or you'll lose balance.

The more supple you are, the

Mini-club check
Use a mini-club about 2ft (60cm) long to check your position at the top of the backswing. When you look over your right shoulder you can easily see the clubhead of a short-shafted club – which you can't with a normal club. If you have an old club ask your local pro to cut it down for you.

Holding the mini-club with the standard grip, take up the posture and address position for a medium iron. Make a backswing; hold your position at the top.

Your position is correct if the shaft points at the target and the back of your left hand is set at the same angle as the clubface.

3 MID POINT
By mid point on the backswing your right arm starts to bend. This opens the clubface. Your rotating left shoulder has pulled your left hip to the right. Your weight moves on to your right foot and the toe of the clubhead points at the sky.

4 MOVE SMOOTHLY
As your upper body continues to rotate, your wrists set – they remain in this position to the top of the backswing. Your left knee moves towards the ball and your weight is now on the inside of your right foot. Let your head move with your body.

5 CLUBHEAD SWINGS HIGH
At the three-quarter point in the backswing, your rotating shoulders, arms and hands have lifted the clubhead well above your head. Your left arm is still reasonably straight while your right arm is bent. Your legs stay flexed.

6 COILED BODY AT TOP
At the top of the backswing your upper body is fully coiled ready to unleash a powerful downswing. Your left arm provides the leverage for pulling the clubhead through the ball. Your upper body has turned about 90° and your hips and knees about 45°.

BE STRAIGHT AT THE TOP

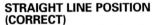

INCORRECT CUPPED POSITION
If your shoulders fail to rotate correctly, and your arms, wrists and hands do not extend fully, the imaginary line is cupped and you slice the shot.

STRAIGHT LINE POSITION (CORRECT)
At the top of the backswing your left arm, left wrist and left hand are joined by an imaginary straight line.

more your head moves naturally as your body rotates. This is fine so long as you keep your eye on the ball.

Your right knee is flexed but not locked, and your lower body supports your upper body as it rotates to the top of the backswing.

TOP OF BACKSWING

By the top of the backswing your upper body has rotated halfway round – about 90° – while your hips, thighs and knees have made a quarter turn – about 45°. Your right arm is considerably bent while your left arm remains reasonably straight.

This is important. If your left arm is either crooked or limp you lose power on the downswing. A straight left arm provides a powerful lever for pulling the clubhead through the ball.

At the top of a good backswing your body feels coiled and ready to unwind, unleashing power on the downswing.

The exact positioning varies depending on the length of the shaft. Although your upper body must always rotate about 90°, the length of your swing alters. You should make a full swing with a wood and a long iron, but only a three-quarter swing with a medium and short iron.

The back of your left wrist and left hand and the clubface are set at the same angle. With a medium iron you make a three-quarter swing – though your upper body still turns 90°.

Allow for a very slight pause at the top of the backswing before starting the downswing. Although this pause shouldn't be long enough to be visible, it lets your body change direction smoothly. A pause also prevents you from rushing the start of the downswing.

RELAX AT ADDRESS

You can't rotate correctly if you're tense at address. Tension can affect most parts of your body. It makes your muscles tighten, which restricts body movement and stops your chest, shoulders and arms from rotating fully.

There are a number of ways to relieve tension. One is to do a few warm-up or stretching exercises before picking up a club. Another is to lift the clubhead just off the ground and waggle your feet at address. This keeps your muscles ticking over and stops them from becoming stiff.

If you still find it difficult to make a full swing, even after a warm-up session, don't try to force one. Not only can this cause injury, it also affects your tempo. Providing your body rotates correctly and you keep your rhythm, a three-quarter backswing is enough until you are able to develop a full swing.

INCORRECT ARCHED POSITION
If the clubhead moves too far inside the ball-to-target line on the backswing, the imaginary line is arched and you produce a hook.

pro tip

Your flat right hand
Using a driver, the palm of your right hand should be flat enough at the top of the backswing to support a few books. Check this by holding your position at the top. Remove the club with your left hand. Is the right palm flat?

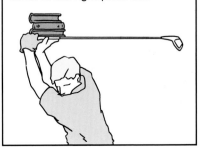

Impact

The impact position is the point during the swing when you're about to strike the ball. It's the moment when – if you swing correctly – the clubhead finally catches up with your hands.

To hit a golf ball both long and straight down the fairway, you must return the clubhead to the ball with two qualities – power and accuracy.

Your body position at impact differs for irons and woods, but ball position and shaft length combine to alter the strike. With woods, no divot is taken as you sweep the ball – which is opposite your left heel – off the fairway or tee peg.

To gain top benefit from an iron club, it's vital to strike the ball first, before taking a small divot. Move the ball towards the centre of your stance as the shaft length shortens.

SQUARE CLUBFACE

There are many different types of correct golf swing – but only one correct impact position. This means returning the clubface squarely to the ball, which leads to straight hitting. Building power is more complicated.

You coil power in the back-swing – this power is stored at the top. As your downswing begins, your lower body starts a weight shift to the left and your shoulders, arms and hands follow, before finally releasing the clubhead at impact.

Being in the proper impact

ONE IMPACT POSITION
Although there are many types of golf swing, there is only one impact position. It's similar to the set-up – the clubface is square to the ball, but the lower body is shifting left.

INCORRECT: NO LOWER BODY MOVEMENT

CLUB STAYS AHEAD
Starting your swing with your shoulders and failing to move your lower body left means that most of your weight stays firmly fixed on the right. You swing the clubface across the line, which closes the clubface and causes a slice.

WRONG: WEIGHT STAYS ON RIGHT

INCORRECT: MOVING AHEAD

EARLY WEIGHT TRANSFER
As you start the downswing, you shift your weight too quickly to the left, and you move ahead of the clubhead. At impact the club has no chance of catching up, usually causing an open clubface – and a push.

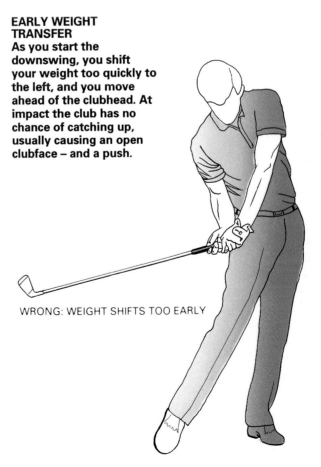

WRONG: WEIGHT SHIFTS TOO EARLY

PRACTISE YOUR HAND POSITION

1 ADDRESS
Stand with knees flexed in your normal address position. Hold out both arms in front of you, as if about to take grip.

2 TOP OF BACKSWING
Leave your left arm straight and swing your right arm to the top of the backswing position. Slowly move your hips back to the left, keeping your knees bent.

3 IMPACT
Look at your hand positions. They should have returned to impact solely through lower body movement. No conscious hand action should be needed.

CORRECT WEIGHT SHIFT THROUGH IMPACT

CLUBHEAD CATCHES UP WITH HANDS
As you start your downswing, your left hip turns to the left – enough to transfer your weight to your left foot. This movement lowers your hands and arms to the mid point position. You should feel very powerful, with both arms loaded with energy. The muscles in your left hip and thigh keep turning smoothly to the left and your right leg and knee follow. Your lower body is taut but springy. The shot does not finish with the strike – your weight continues to your left side, letting your upper body turn and face the target. This movement brings your head up to watch the ball's flight.

pro tip

USE AN UMBRELLA

Drive an umbrella into the ground and set up as normal with the outside of your left foot (right foot for left-handers) touching the umbrella. Make your usual swing.

You're in the correct position at impact if your left knee touches the umbrella, but the space remains between your hip and the umbrella.

position ensures that you achieve maximum distance and the correct trajectory. If you're out of position, you're likely to hit fat (behind the ball) or thin (halfway up).

HIP ACTION

To hit squarely at impact, you must start the downswing with the correct hip action by turning your hips smoothly left.

Feel as if your hips pull the arms and hands down until the mid point of the downswing, when your arms should be loaded with power. Your shoulders send power to your arms, the arms to the hands and your hands pass it on to the clubhead.

If everything else is as it should be, the clubface is square on contact. Don't try to control the clubface at this point – it's moving far too quickly.

At impact, the clubhead, arms and hands form a straight line, although your position is not identical to the one you adopt at set-up. This is because your lower body carries on turning to the left, so that your weight shifts fully from your right side. Keep your head steady.

Remember that you haven't finished playing the shot when you strike the ball – it's important to make a full follow through.

Video evidence

If you can't go to a tournament to see the professionals at work first hand, television is the next best medium to study their swings. Use a video to record the event and then analyse the players' actions.

The slow motion and freeze frame functions are invaluable for picking out the key parts in the swing and examining them in detail.

Stop the action at the full extent of the takeaway to see if a player has taken the club back on, inside or outside the line. Freeze the top of backswing and impact positions as well.

It's useful to get hold of a video camera to record your own swing, so you can compare your action to the greats. This gives you an idea of what you should be working on to improve your game.

CRITICAL IMPACT

▲ Johnny Miller's major winning impact.

▲ Andrew Murray – winner European Open 1989.

Although your eyes can't freeze and capture an impact position like a camera can, you should still be able to see the movements of the body and club in the striking zone. Whether a pro is an all time great like Johnny Miller, or a lesser light with one Euro Tour win like Andrew Murray, the impact positions are almost identical.

Look for a drive with the legs and a clearing of the left side. Although the lower body has opened up, the shoulders are still parallel with the target line. Watch also for the head staying behind the ball and the hands and blade square to the target – all vital for controlled hitting.

Weight transfer

There's more than one way to strike a golf ball well, but if you want to hit good shots on a regular basis you must transfer your weight correctly during the swing. With a good weight shift power flows smoothly from your body through to the club and the ball.

For a full shot, a little more than half your weight should be on your right foot at the top of the backswing. As you start the downswing your weight gradually shifts towards the target. And when you complete your followthrough, you must have almost all of your weight on your left foot.

You may get away with a less than classical action. Many great players in the past have prospered with an unorthodox swing – Arnold Palmer and Lee Trevino are two perfect examples. But correct weight transfer is an essential ingredient of every successful golf swing – once you've got it right, don't tamper with it.

ADDRESSING THE PROBLEM

Take the first steps to correct weight transfer before you swing the club. At address make sure your weight is equally distributed on both feet. It's much easier to build a good swing if the foundations are solid.

Any fault is likely to cause you misery. If too much of your weight is on the left side it's extremely difficult to make a wide backswing. This is likely to restrict your weight transfer – and perhaps even cause a destructive reverse pivot where you lean towards the target on the backswing.

If you have more than half of your

THE WEIGHTING GAME
Whatever your age, sex or build, making sure your weight distribution is correct benefits your game. Most of your weight must be on the left foot through impact. This action helps you hit down and through the ball – essential if you want the satisfaction and enjoyment of hitting crisply struck iron shots.

WEIGHT WATCHERS

1 SHARED EQUALLY
Make sure your weight is evenly distributed – position your feet about shoulder width apart for a solid base. If you get it right at address you make life easier when parts start moving. Note how the arrows show the small amount of sway needed for good weight transfer.

2 HALFWAY BACK
Sweeping the club back long and wide naturally pulls your weight away from the ball. From an evenly balanced position at address, more of your weight is on the right than the left – even at this early stage in the swing.

5 CONTROLLED POWER
A good weight shift helps generate power at impact. The left leg is firm and supporting more than half your body weight. Both arms are fully extended, driving the clubhead low towards the target. The ball is propelled forward on a penetrating flight.

6 RIGHT TO LEFT
The body faces the target and the left leg is straight – note the position of the right foot indicating how little weight is on that side. When the weight transfer is as smooth as this you can maintain perfect control from start to finish.

3 TOP OF BACKSWING
Notice how the head has tilted slightly to allow an uninhibited shoulder turn, yet it has moved sideways very little from its original position. If your head does move too far, there's every chance something else in the swing has also done so.

4 SMOOTH DOWN
The shift of weight back towards the target should start before you pull the club down. This helps set the club on the correct path down into the ball and also guards against flailing with your hands only.

weight on the right side at address there's every chance you sway too far away from the ball on the backswing.

RIGHT FROM THE START

Your backswing is the key move. A wide takeaway acts as a trigger to help you transfer your weight on to the right side. Achieve this and you naturally pull your upper body into a coiled position.

Your right leg acts as a brace at the top of the backswing. The leg should be comfortably flexed yet firm to resist any tendency to sway backwards. This puts you in a strong position to support your body weight.

Think of tempo at the top and make sure you transfer your weight smoothly towards the left side on the downswing. As well as promoting a pure strike, it helps you achieve the classic balanced followthrough so recognizable with good golfers.

If you leave your weight trailing behind, you probably find yourself scooping at impact. It's impossible to strike correctly if you're toppling

back away from the ball. The likelihood is you hit plenty of thinned shots.

When you analyse your swing, remember that weight transfer is not the same as a sway. It's important to understand the difference between the two.

A very slight sway away from the ball on the backswing is fine and encourages weight transfer. So if you study your swing in a mirror or on video, don't feel anxious if you do sway a little on the backswing. The important point is that your weight shifts towards the ball on the way down. An excessive sway is potentially disastrous – it's definitely a problem that must be addressed.

TRANSFER TRAINING

A simple exercise can help you appreciate the importance of weight transfer. When you're next on the practice ground, adopt your normal stance with your weight equally distributed on both feet. A 5 iron is the best club to use.

Hit a couple of shots while making a deliberate attempt to keep your

feet firmly planted on the ground – almost as if there's glue on the soles of your shoes. This makes it impossible to transfer your weight correctly during the swing – particularly through impact. You're certain to hit al-most every bad shot imaginable so don't continue this drill for too long.

Now revert to a more orthodox action. Concentrate on transferring your weight on to the right foot on the backswing and on to the left on the downswing. Straight away you should strike the ball with more power and authority.

pro tip

Supporting role
An accurate way to check you're in a good followthrough position is to try to stand on your left leg immediately after you complete your swing. If you can, it means your balance is good and that you're transferring your weight correctly both on the downswing and through impact.

TEMPO AND RHYTHM

Almost all golfers are aware that tempo and rhythm are the keys to success, but few are able to achieve this distinctive quality. It is not a question of how fast or how slow you swing the club but learning how to swing the club at the right speed for you. Nick Faldo's swing has been rhythmical throughout his career, helping him become one of the world's top players.

During his heyday in the late '70s and early '80s Tom Watson was recognised as the greatest player in the world by press, players and public alike.

Tempo and rhythm

To be a consistent striker of the ball your swing must have good tempo and rhythm. Tempo is the speed at which you swing the club while rhythm is its fluency.

Good tempo and rhythm allow every moving part of your body to co-ordinate as a single unit. Although your head, shoulders, arms, hands, hips, knees and feet have their own function, they must work together during the swing. If your tempo is too fast or erratic, this doesn't happen and you don't make a solid strike.

Even if your set-up is perfect and you swing the clubhead along the correct path, you only play effective golf when your tempo and rhythm are relaxed and smooth.

DEVELOPING YOUR TEMPO

Most players with poor tempo and rhythm swing the club too fast in a vain attempt to work up power and distance. A quick or rushed swing doesn't allow each individual movement enough time to perform its task and your action is jerky.

To find your natural tempo and rhythm concentrate on swinging the club smoothly. Start with a half swing. Only when you achieve a solid, consistent strike should you lengthen your swing to three-quarter and then full.

Developing your ideal tempo and rhythm takes practice as well as natural ability. Once they improve you can build a repeatable swing.

It is vital you concentrate on keeping a good tempo and rhythm when playing a round. Once you've

SWINGING SMOOTHLY
Good tempo and rhythm allow each individual movement within your swing to work correctly and help produce a perfect swing path. If your swing is too quick your body hasn't enough time to rotate properly and the clubface isn't square at impact.

UNDERSTANDING TEMPO AND RHYTHM

1 TAKEAWAY
The takeaway dictates the speed of the swing. If you rush it, the rest of your swing becomes too fast and erratic. Concentrate on taking the club away smoothly.

2 THE BACKSWING
Your backswing must have a smooth and even rhythm. This allows your hands, arms and shoulders to move as one, and helps you to feel the clubhead throughout the stroke.

3 TOP OF BACKSWING
Allow for a slight pause at the top of the backswing to ensure that you complete it. This prevents you from rushing the downswing.

selected the club to fit into your game plan, your only thought should be making a smooth swing. Visualize your swing as a whole. Avoid analysing any specific movement within your swing just as you blot out hazards on the fairway.

RECOVERING LOST TEMPO

No player – even leading professionals – consistently maintains perfect tempo and rhythm. Regaining your timing isn't difficult – as long as you go back to basics.

Once you establish a regular distance with each club, recover lost tempo and rhythm by playing to a shorter target. Reduce the distance you try to send each shot by about one-third. This automatically slows your swing down, allowing each body movement enough time to function.

By slowing down and reducing the length of your swing you

4 THE DOWNSWING
The downswing must have the same tempo and swing path as the backswing. To help you swing the club on the same line, the start of the downswing must be smooth.

5 IMPACT
To make a solid strike your tempo and rhythm must be perfect. Your swing movements must co-ordinate properly so that the clubface is square at impact.

6 FOLLOWTHROUGH
Your swing slows down as smoothly as it increased at takeaway. Good tempo and rhythm look effortless and should become natural and consistent with regular practice.

SHORTEN YOUR SWING

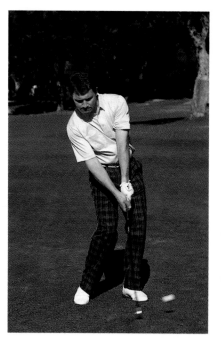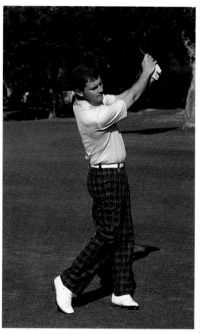

One of the best ways to improve – as well as understand – tempo and rhythm is to practise a three- **quarter swing. By shortening your swing you slow it down and it is easier for its individual movements** **to co-ordinate correctly. A three-quarter swing also increases clubhead feel.**

lessen tension and develop greater clubhead feel. You also hit the ball further than you expect because you achieve a more solid strike.

With a slower action it is easier to identify any faults in your set-up and swing – and then correct them. From here you can increase your tempo until your swing combines rhythm, consistency and power.

FEET TOGETHER

Another exercise for finding good tempo and rhythm is to hit the ball with your feet together. Because your centre of gravity is higher than with a normal stance you must reduce the speed, length and power of your swing to avoid losing balance.

The best way to understand and appreciate tempo and rhythm is to watch top players – either at tournaments or on television. Although they all swing the club differently their tempo and rhythm are perfect.

Take an image of their swing on to the practice range or course and try to copy it. It's amazing how you can improve your own swing – and your game – by trying to imitate top players.

REDUCE YOUR DISTANCE

If your swing is too fast, slow it down by reducing the distance you try to hit each shot. For example, if you normally expect to strike a 5 iron about 150yd (136m), go to the practice ground and aim at a target 100yd (91m) away. This makes you reduce the length, speed and power of your normal swing, and helps you develop a smoother action.

Faldo's perfect tempo

A good golf swing is one you can repeat, even under the tightest pressure. Perhaps the finest swinger in modern golf is Nick Faldo.

One reason why the Hertfordshire golfer keeps getting it right is because his tempo (speed of swing) remains the same, whatever the shot, whatever the club, whatever the situation.

Throughout his career, tempo has been one of Faldo's strongest features and has been the framework of his machine-like accuracy.

Because he keeps an even tempo in every situation, Nick removes much of the pressure that he faces in every tournament.

SAME SPEED

The secret of Faldo's swing tempo is simple – he makes sure it's the same for every club in the bag. From the 1 iron to the 9 iron and the woods, it's hard to detect a change in his movements or the speed of his swing.

Most tournament players – and Faldo is no exception – look as if they play golf in third gear. They always seem to have something in reserve and never give the ball a massive thump. This is because they know that it is clubhead speed, and not body speed, that determines how far the ball travels.

CONSISTENCY

Consistent tempo is the way to achieve consistent clubhead speed. If your tempo – and so the clubhead speed – is the same with each club, you can be confident of knowing how far you regularly hit each club. Your course management is then much more effective.

1 SET-UP
At address, Faldo adopts a very comfortable and relaxed position. His toes point outward, with flexed knees and body weight evenly distributed. The hands and arms hang naturally. Every part of Faldo's body is geared to a smooth swing.

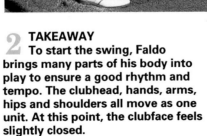

2 TAKEAWAY
To start the swing, Faldo brings many parts of his body into play to ensure a good rhythm and tempo. The clubhead, hands, arms, hips and shoulders all move as one unit. At this point, the clubface feels slightly closed.

3 TOP OF BACKSWING
As his upper body completes its 90° turn, Faldo's knees remain flexed. His weight has shifted easily to his right side and the clubhead is square, on line and pointing at the target.

A changeable tempo gives different results. If you produce less clubhead speed with a 3 iron than you do with a 5 iron, it's very likely that you hit the 5 iron as far as the longer-shafted club. This means you cannot know your limits with either club and judge your play accordingly, as the top players do.

GOOD RHYTHM

Although the golf swing becomes a little longer as the club length-

ens, your rhythm must always remain the same.

Balance is the key to good rhythm. Practice with your eyes closed to help you concentrate on every detail of the swing rather than letting your attention focus on the hit.

Keep your swing steady. Consistent golf depends on different parts of your body regularly slotting into their correct position – any sudden movement prevents this, making you miss-hit the ball.

4 DOWNSWING
The left hip starts the downswing by moving to the left. Faldo's weight now begins its shift to the left side.

This classic position shows the immense leverage created by the hands and arms pulling the club down. It delays releasing the clubhead, so that the power is stored until the last possible moment. Faldo can now be sure of maximum distance.

5 IMPACT
The left hip continues to clear to the left, letting Faldo's hands and arms swing the club through the ball. His head is perfectly still. Nick holds his lower body back – although at impact 90% of his weight has transferred to his left side.

6 THROUGHSWING
As his upper body turns fully to the left, Faldo swings through to a composed throughswing position. His right side is pulled round to a finish on the tip of his right toe. His head swivels to watch the ball.

Watch yourself on video
To check closely if you are keeping to the same tempo with every club in the bag, it's a good idea to team up with some other players and video your swing. With the camera directly in front of you, make a full swing with all your clubs, from driver through to wedge.

Make sure that your whole swing is visible in the viewfinder. If your tempo is consistent, it's hard to spot the difference between your swings, as they have the same measured pace with each club.

If you don't have access to a video camera, the phone book lists firms with hire facilities.

PREPARATION IS VITAL

How often do you go to the first tee without any preparation? If you were to allow thirty to forty minutes for practice it would make all the difference, perhaps allowing you to start the round immediately instead of using the first six holes as a warm-up. Last but not least, if you really want to lower your scores then take lessons from a professional. There are so many different aspects of play to learn that skilled tuition can make all the difference.

Tom Watson's all-round game
improved and his swing under
pressure became more reliable
thanks to help from Byron Nelson,
a former giant of the game.

Preparing for a competition

There's no such thing as a dead certainty in golf. Good rounds crop up when you least expect them, and nightmares can unfold just when you really felt it was going to be your day.

Tour professionals experience similar peaks and troughs. The difference is that pros go through the same pre-tournament routine every week. In many ways, this must make it all the more frustrating, but they at least give themselves a chance of performing to the best of their ability.

Competition preparation is essential if you want to do yourself justice. There's more than one way to get ready for a competition, so try to find an overall approach that works for you. Certain points are a feature of every successful routine. It's a good idea to be aware of them, because at the end of the day it's important to be able to say you did your best – win or lose.

AWAY FROM HOME

Preparation doesn't start on the day itself. There's plenty to do before the day of the competition – particularly if you're playing away from your home club. It's normal for the organizers of any event to grant all competitors courtesy of the course for the week leading up to the event.

Try to take advantage of this whenever possible because it greatly boosts your chances of winning. Most golfers find a course easier when they've seen it before. Club selection is often

GIVE IT YOUR BEST SHOT
Make the most of the hour or so immediately before your tee time. These valuable minutes often make the difference between success and failure. Spend some time on the practice ground. Work your way through the bag building the sort of rhythm into your swing that you can repeat on the 1st tee. Too many club golfers go into battle totally unprepared. When you're not ready, there will be days when your game clicks into place. But there are likely to be many more when your chances of winning are severely dented through making a frustrating poor start.

READY FOR THE BIG EVENT

If a competition matters to you, it makes sense to give yourself the best possible chance of winning. There isn't a single professional golfer in the world who plays a competitive round without first preparing thoroughly. Before you see them thump their first shot straight down the middle, they've probably been peppering the targets on the practice ground.

Most professionals go through the same routine every week. You're unlikely to have as much time on your hands as a professional – and it's almost certain that your club doesn't have the same facilities as a tour venue, but there are ways of making the most of those precious few minutes before you tee off.

POINTS TO WORK ON

This is no time to make a swing change. Ensure the fundamentals are there, but don't become bogged down with too many theories on the golf swing. The most crucial part of your game to work on is rhythm and tempo – you need to find a pace of swing that you can take on to the course.

Start with some gentle chips to several targets. Try to gain an overall feel for each shot and don't worry too much if every one doesn't finish stone dead. Then move up gradually through the clubs in your bag. Don't feel you have to hit a shot with every club – select three or four of those you're most comfortable with.

Finish off by hitting a few shots with your driver. Swing within yourself and remember, there are no prizes for trying to smash the cover off the ball. This is likely to upset the rhythm you've developed over the last half hour and entirely defeats the object of practising before the round.

pro tip

The finishing touch

Round off every practice session with a spot of putting. If possible, try to find a flat area on the putting green and concentrate on the medium length putts and the occasional one from long range. Try to avoid practising the short putts – they're easily missed and can undermine your confidence.

Grip the putter lightly in your hands and stand comfortably. Work at building a smooth stroke and trying to gain a good feel for distance. Try not to think too much about technique – this can often cause tension.

Again, don't be upset if the putts don't drop – you should stroll from the practice green in a relaxed frame of mind. In many ways this is the ideal winding down exercise to a pre-competition practice session.

more accurate second time around and you can also gain a feel for the greens, which may be different to those you're used to.

ROUTE MAP

Pick up a course planner when you're there and study it on the way round. There are several points you need to look out for, such as hidden bunkers or ditches. You also need to identify the danger holes, where you can easily drive into trouble, and those where you feel there's an opportunity to attack.

Often forgotten is the route you intend taking to the course. Make sure you know how to get there and how long it takes – don't rely on a last minute glance at the map and a frantic dash down the motorway. Struggling to make your tee off time is the worst preparation in the world.

Getting ready for a competition at your home course – the monthly medal or Captain's Weekend for example – takes on a different form. You should know when to play safe and when to attack – club selection and reading the greens are unlikely to cause problems.

EQUIPMENT INSPECTION

Check that your clubs are clean, particularly if you've recently put in lots of practice. Having hit plenty of balls it's quite possible that your clubs are caked in a layer of dry grass and mud. This looks unsightly and more importantly reduces the amount of spin you can apply on the ball.

Make sure your golf bag is well stocked with balls, tees and anything else you might need. And don't make the mistake of taking more than 14 clubs on to the course. You also need to make sure that none of your clubs is missing. For instance, it's easy to

leave your putter behind – particularly if you've been working on your stroke at home.

ACCEPT THE BAD DAYS

Even the best preparation in the world is no guarantee of success. When your own worst nightmare unfolds before your eyes, take heart from the fact that you don't earn a living hitting golf balls.

When professionals have their off days they generally accept them more favourably than their on-screen image suggests. Most are seldom as unhappy as they appear.

'Television is the reason golf has this serious image,' said Fuzzy Zoeller at the 1990 US Open. 'They only show the leaders on television – those guys are tensed up. Those of us in the back of the field, we're having a good time.' There lies a message for every amateur having a bad day.

READY, STEADY, GO

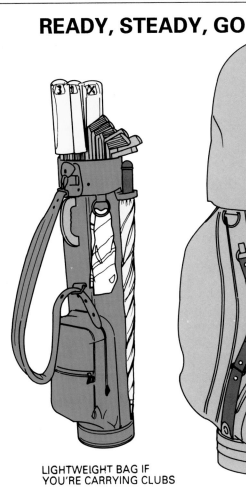

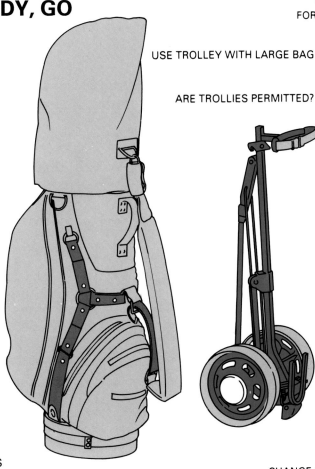

LIGHTWEIGHT BAG IF
YOU'RE CARRYING CLUBS

USE TROLLEY WITH LARGE BAG

ARE TROLLIES PERMITTED?

WATERPROOFS
FOR BAD WEATHER

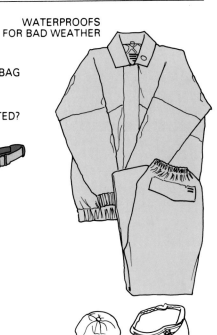

SPARE GLOVES FOR RAIN AND HOT
WEATHER – SWAP WHEN DAMP

CHANGE OF CLOTHES
HANDY FOR AFTERNOON ROUND

FORMAL WEAR USUALLY
NEEDED FOR DINNER
AND PRESENTATION

ON COURSE TO CONQUER

Doing well at a tournament away from your home club is a truly satisfying experience and there's no greater proof that your game is in good shape. It's generally harder to win away than it is at home, so in many ways it's these tournaments that you need to prepare for most.

If you're used to pulling your clubs rather than carrying them, make a quick call to the secretary or professional at the away club and find out if they allow trollies. Some clubs ban them in winter, or at other times of the year when major re-seeding of the course has taken place. If this is the case and you turn up with your pro size golf bag, you're in for a hard time carrying it for 18 holes, let alone 36. If you haven't managed to persuade a close friend or relative to caddie for you, it's better to pack your lightweight bag just in case. This is also worth doing when you use an electrically powered trolley – you never know when the battery might go flat.

DRESS FOR SUCCESS

Be prepared for changes in the weather. Pack your waterproofs and also bring a change of clothes for the afternoon round. This is worth while whether it's pouring with rain or extremely hot because it's always refreshing to have clean clothes to change into. Pulling on a soaking wet pair of socks and trousers is hardly the most pleasant start to an afternoon of golf.

Most competitions are followed by a dinner and presentation in the evening, so bring along a jacket and tie for the formal part of the day. Always make a point of doing this – there aren't too many clubs around that allow you into the dining room if you're improperly dressed. After all, you should go along to every competition with the attitude that you might be fortunate – and well prepared – enough to collect a prize.

Overcoming nerves

The 1st tee in an important competition, or the 18th tee on a good score, are two fine examples of a pressure situation. Waves of emotion wash over you – nerves are often high on the list.

Every professional would freely admit to feeling a touch of nerves on plenty of occasions during their career. Don't think for a minute that you're the only golfer who suffers from anxiety.

However, when you see top golfers hit good shots at tense moments, it's easy to assume they can't be feeling the pressure. This is not true – they simply hide it better than others and have learned to overcome their nerves.

You need to develop the same steely ability.

Excitement often comes hand in hand with nervousness. There's nothing wrong with this, provided you don't let it overtake you. This is where golf differs enormously from most other sports.

Think of an Olympic sprinter. Moments before the off, athletes do everything possible to charge themselves up. They rely on an explosion of energy the split second the starter's gun fires.

However, in a pressure situation on the golf course you need to keep your emotions in check and almost psyche yourself down. It's natural for your heart to beat faster,

STOCK SHOT
Your 1st tee shot is unlike any other because it can set the mood for the entire round. Hit a good one and your confidence soars and nerves seem to evaporate. If you hit a poor shot, the next is harder and your nerves are no better – a touch of humiliation is also thrown in. With so much hinging on the 1st shot, it's vital you choose a club you're confident of hitting well. If this means taking a long iron rather than your driver, don't feel embarrassed to do just that.

LOOK BACK ON THE HIGHLIGHTS

THINK POSITIVE

In every good score there are certain to be times in the round where you played a shot, or a hole, exceptionally well. So why should it be any different at the end of the round? The ability is there on the day, but your doubts and nerves sometimes let you down at crucial stages.

One excellent way to overcome nerves towards the end of the round is to cast your mind back a few holes.

Remember where you splashed out of a greenside bunker to save par – or perhaps fired in an approach shot stone dead for birdie. By running over these highlights again in your mind, you develop a positive attitude. Once you achieve this, you're mentally more prepared to hit good shots under pressure. You start concentrating on how well you've been playing, rather than worrying about what might go wrong.

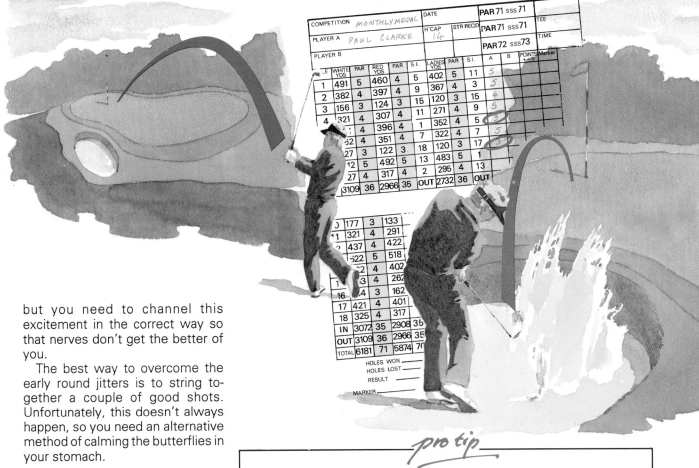

COMPETITION	MONTHLY MEDAL		DATE			PAR 71 sss 71			TEE
PLAYER A	PAUL CLARKE		H'CAP 14	STR REC'D		PAR 71 sss 71			TIME
PLAYER B						PAR 72 sss 73			

LE	WHITE YDS	PAR	RED YDS	PAR	S.I.	LADIES YDS	PAR	S.I.	A	B	POINTS +-0	Marker
1	491	5	460	4	5	402	5	11	5			
2	382	4	397	4	9	367	4	3	5			
3	156	3	124	3	15	120	3	15	4			
4	321	4	307	4	11	271	4	9	5			
	4	396	4	1	352	4	5	5			
62	4	351	4	7	322	4	7	5			
27	3	122	3	18	120	3	17	3			
12	5	492	5	13	483	5					
27	4	317	4	2	295	4	13				
3109	36	2966	35	OUT	2732	36	OUT			

	177	3	133		
11	321	4	291		
	437	4	422		
522	5	518		
2	4	402		
3	4	262		
16	4	3	162		
17	421	4	401		
18	325	4	317		
IN	3072	35	2908	35	
OUT	3109	36	2966	35	
TOTAL	6181	71	5874	70	

HOLES WON _____
HOLES LOST _____
RESULT _____
MARKER _____

but you need to channel this excitement in the correct way so that nerves don't get the better of you.

The best way to overcome the early round jitters is to string together a couple of good shots. Unfortunately, this doesn't always happen, so you need an alternative method of calming the butterflies in your stomach.

STAY COOL

It's important not to be in a hurry to get away from a crowded 1st tee. Give yourself time and if you have a pre-shot routine, be sure to carry it out.

Once on the course, you must resist the temptation to rush. Many golfers practically run to their ball as they near the end of a cracking good round – particularly when feeling nervous. Make a conscious effort to walk slowly, because in an exciting situation this probably clips you down to your normal pace.

This has a knock-on effect when you arrive at your ball. You have time to think straight rather than making a hasty decision. You should also be able to maintain your normal swing tempo instead of allowing it to quicken.

pro tip

Thinking straight

Nerves tend to muddle your train of thought. A challenging shot – such as firing over a tree – can have a disastrous effect on your score and confidence.

Use constructively the time it takes you to walk to your ball. Weigh up the options in your mind, decide on the shot and then run through the key points. You need plenty of height to avoid the tree so you must hit down on the ball. From a distance you should also gain a fair indication of the club you need.

This allows you to make most of the decisions before you address the ball, so there's less to worry about when you get there. This helps you concentrate because fewer doubts are running through your mind as you stand to the ball.

1987 OPEN,
MUIRFIELD – 72nd HOLE

BUNKERED 2ND
DESTROYS
CHAMPIONSHIP
HOPES

FALDO –
ROCK SOLID
DOWN THE
HOME STRETCH

AZINGER –
WOBBLES AT
CRUCIAL MOMENT

Six million dollar blow out

The 1989 US Open provided a good example of how pressure affects golfers in different ways, and how nerves can play a major part in the final outcome.

Going into the last round Tom Kite held a 3 stroke lead over the field. Alas, the pressure of the final round took its toll. Kite slumped to a catastrophic 78 – a round that included a triple bogey and two double bogeys.

The collapse left the disconsolate Kite languishing in a tie for 9th place. 'My golf stank,' said the man who has accumulated over six million dollars but no Majors.

Meanwhile, Curtis Strange compiled a steady level par round of 70 to complete a 1 stroke victory. While others faltered, his golf was rock solid under the most intense pressure the game can inflict.

There was very little between Kite and Strange throughout the tournament. In the end, the only factor that could separate them was their ability to perform under pressure.

Strange marches on

Kite plummets

DOWN TO THE WIRE

Described by Jack Nicklaus as 'one of the best holes anywhere', the 18th at Muirfield is never anything less than a stiff test of nerve. Add to this the pressure of the final hole in a major championship and something or someone is bound to crack.

In the last round of the 1987 Open Championship, Nick Faldo displayed immense concentration and determination in producing a round of 72. The rock solid 4 he made on the last was his 18th consecutive par of the round and made him leader in the clubhouse.

Close behind in the final group out on the course, Paul Azinger needed a par on the last to tie. Already showing signs of wobbling on previous holes, Azinger dumped his 2nd shot into the bunker guarding the left side of the green and failed to get up and down in 2, thus waving goodbye to his hopes of a first Major.

When you're under pressure, stay steady and don't try anything beyond your abilities. As Faldo showed, concentration, coolness and par golf can be just as effective as a birdie blitz if you're to win.

Create a good impression

Every golfer is keen to impress on the 1st tee – particularly when there are plenty of onlookers. It's likely to increase a feeling of nervousness rather than soothe it. Not only must you expect this, you need to know how to cope with it if you're to fire away a good drive.

Talk yourself into hitting a good shot. Tell yourself to demonstrate to the spectators exactly what you can do.

It's not easy and in a sense it's a mild form of showing off. This may not be your style, but if you start worrying about what might go wrong, then it's almost certain something will.

PLAYING UNDER PRESSURE

MAINTAIN RHYTHM AND TEMPO

On the final morning of the 1970 US Open, Tony Jacklin found a message from Tom Weiskopf taped to the door of his locker. It consisted of one word only – tempo. This sums up the importance of maintaining your normal tempo and rhythm when the pressure is on. Jacklin was leading the tournament – Weiskopf knew tempo was the key to his friend's success.

Learn a valuable lesson from Weiskopf's reminder. When a golfer gets nervous the first reaction is usually a quickening of the swing – this is probably the biggest single cause of mistakes. When the heat is on, keep your tempo smooth and your rhythm the same for every shot. Once you've set up correctly, make this your main swing thought – it's far more important to a successful shot than many golfers realize.

KEEP TEMPO SMOOTH

You're not the only one

When you feel nervous it's easy to think it's happening only to you. Everywhere you look there seem to be golfers strolling about blissfully unaware of the pressures of holding together a good score.

Think again. Anyone who has ever held a golf club has at some stage felt nervous about knocking a little white ball into a hole only slightly larger. There is nothing wrong with feeling this way, as long as you learn through experience how to cope.

The fear of failure strikes more often than most golfers would care to admit. It's perhaps the hardest form of nerves to cope with, because it can be so destructive.

When things do go wrong, don't dwell on your misfortune. Every golfer has made a complete mess of a brilliant round. There's no more depressing feeling in golf because you feel you've buckled under the pressure of your own worst fears.

It's often said that you need to experience failure before you can truly know how to win. The key is learning lessons from the bad rounds by identifying where and why you made mistakes.

Draw great comfort from the fact that if you succeed once when your nerve ends are jangling, it's a lot easier to cope when you're next in a similar situation.

Ronan Rafferty knows that winning is never easy. It's a severe examination of nerves – he is one professional to pass the test.

After a series of near misses, Rafferty finally triumphed in the 1989 Italian Open. Having been in similar positions before, Rafferty had learned from his mistakes and could hold his nerve.

Choosing the right teacher

Most golfers have had at least one lesson from a professional. It may be the beginner learning the fundamentals from day one, or perhaps the experienced player attempting to iron out a fault that's crept in recently.

You should be looking for certain qualities in your ideal teacher whether you've just taken up the game or are already an accomp-

lished player.

You don't need to be a member of a club to have a lesson with the resident professional. Also remember that the assistant pro charges less than the club pro himself. He's just as qualified to teach – though less experienced.

Talk to your friends for possible recommendations – someone may

BEST ADVICE
Liam White of the England amateur squad listens to words of wisdom from the well known teacher John Stirling – even the most accomplished players never stop learning about the golf swing. If you too can find a teacher you like, and more importantly understand, you have someone who can analyse, improve and check your game for years to come.

Lyle's lesson

Sandy Lyle's early association with golf is well documented – he reputedly first strode the fairways at the age of just four. His record is the classic example of being taught the right habits as a junior and seeking regular advice ever since.

From the moment Lyle took up the game his swing was closely scrutinized by his father Alex – long time professional at Hawkstone Park and until the late '80s his one and only teacher.

But even for someone as talented as Lyle, golf has it's ups and downs. When things went wrong, rather than search for advice elsewhere he first looked to his father for the cure – the one person who knew his swing inside out.

Only between late 1988 and 1990 – in the middle of a terrible slump – did he seek advice from various other golfing gurus. But it was the combination of Lyle and Lyle that laid the foundations of a game that won Sandy two majors – the Open Championship and US Masters.

have had a lesson from a professional who made the golf swing easy to understand. You certainly don't want a teacher who baffles you with too much technical jargon.

THE RIGHT CHOICE

Every professional has their own style of teaching, so always book just one lesson on your first visit to a club. You can then judge whether or not you feel the pro is right for you.

It's not a good idea to take the trouble of making a block booking only to discover later that you don't get on with the pro – or worse still don't understand any of the instructions you're given.

It's essential you respect your teacher and have faith in what you're taught. You need to place yourself in the hands of your teacher and trust the advice given. You can then walk away from the lesson feeling you've achieved something and keen to work on the theories on the practice ground.

If you don't believe in the advice of a teacher you're wasting your money. While it's important to discuss the technical aspects of the swing, don't contradict your teacher with lines from the textbook.

You soon know when a teacher is suitable because the lessons are enjoyable. You feel relaxed over the ball rather than nervous and all the instructions make sense rather than confusing the issue.

LONG TERM LEARNING

It's a good idea to stay with a teacher once you find one you feel confident with. If you have booked a series of lessons the professional probably has a logical programme – objectives set out over the long term to improve your game.

Don't expect a miraculous transformation – one lesson alone is unlikely to result in a marked improvement in your game. If changes are being made to your swing, you may have to accept that your game often worsens before you see an upturn.

Nick Faldo is a classic example. After he decided to remodel his swing at the end of 1983, he went through two or three years of sheer torment as he struggled to find any

GROUP THERAPY

Anders Forsbrand discusses techniques with a group of England amateur internationals staying at Valderrama in Spain for a week of practice. It gives them a great opportunity to bounce ideas off players of similar ability.

You can take part in group lessons as well as on a one-to-one basis. This format can be ideal for a group of raw beginners who may feel nervous on their own –

or at the other end of the scale for a team of top amateurs.

While very few club golfers are lucky enough to receive private tuition from a European Tour professional, there are more and more golf schools which create a similar set-up to provide group tuition. Alternatively, you should be able to organize group lessons with friends under the guidance of the pro at your local club.

PUTTING THEORY INTO PRACTICE

When you're receiving lessons from a professional it's important to grab the earliest opportunity to practise what your teacher preaches. Don't follow up a lesson by leaving it two weeks before you set foot on a golf course again – you may lose sight of your objectives.

Work on the specific points talked about in your lesson so that there's a definite purpose to your practice. Also give yourself time to think between shots

and analyse what you're doing. Never rush your shots – it's not a race to see who can hit the most balls.

Make the effort to develop a pre-shot routine – one that you can take on to the course with you. This varies greatly from one golfer to another but you should not delay play. You may find that two looks at the hole and a waggle of the club is the pre-shot routine that works for you. Whatever system you choose to adopt it's an excellent way of focusing your mind on every shot.

sort of consistency. Only then did the hard work start to pay dividends – Faldo's new swing ran like clockwork under the most intense pressure.

Never chop and change from one teacher to another – you may find yourself working on too many parts of the swing. The teaching methods of one professional may well contradict those of another.

Receiving conflicting advice from more than one person is the shortest route to confusion and misery on the course.

REGULAR CHECK-UP

If you're playing well it's still worth booking the occasional lesson with your regular teacher – even if only once every month. This ensures that

you're working on the correct moves and also that no technical flaws are creeping into your swing.

Your teacher should also be good at instilling confidence into your game – telling you you're swinging well and hitting the ball solidly. Confirmation that you're doing the right things in practice is one of the most valuable functions a teacher can perform.

DRESS REGULATIONS

Even though you're only having a lesson rather than playing a competitive round, you still need to dress correctly. It's not simply a question of keeping up appearances – wearing the wrong type of clothing can hinder your performance.

Ideally you should always wear proper golf shoes – trainers are fine if the ground is dry but in wet conditions you're likely to lose your balance every time you swing the club. Wear a loose fitting shirt and pullover to enable you to swing freely.

Also bring with you an extra layer of clothing – remember you're standing still for as long as an hour and are bound to feel the cold more than when you're walking around the course. Don't bring your thickest winter skiing jacket though – it's impossible to swing the club properly if you're wearing bulky clothing.

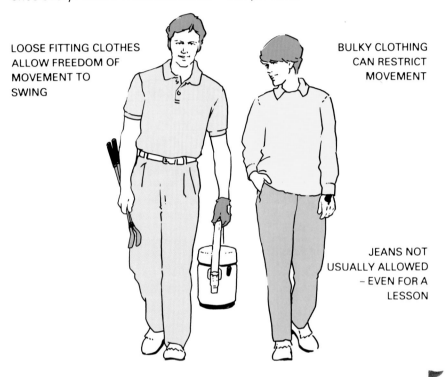

LOOSE FITTING CLOTHES ALLOW FREEDOM OF MOVEMENT TO SWING

BULKY CLOTHING CAN RESTRICT MOVEMENT

JEANS NOT USUALLY ALLOWED – EVEN FOR A LESSON

Keep it in the family

With golf experts abounding in almost every corner of every club in the country, many players still turn to the person they know best for advice.

Professional Elizabeth Quelhas of France is a regular player on the WPG European Tour. Her regular practice partner and tutor is her brother – also a professional golfer – who knows Elizabeth's swing as well as anyone.

The benefit of having the same teacher for several years is that you have someone who becomes familiar with your swing. Any faults – no matter how small – can be more easily identified and put right.

Video your game

The video camera is an effective tool to help improve your golf. Some club professionals use video as a teaching aid in lessons for the amateur golfer. And tournament pros may occasionally analyse their swing on screen.

A video camera is expensive to buy. But to hire one for a day can prove to be real value for money – particularly if you share the cost between a group of friends. Practice should be a rewarding experience – not a chore – and a video camera helps you make the most of your time on the range.

When you watch yourself in action your swing is there before your eyes, instead of being just an image in your mind. You can study your technique in depth, freezing the frames to build a picture of what you're trying to achieve. Seeing an improvement boosts your confidence and this is soon reflected on the course.

Normally it's difficult to correct a fault in golf, even if you know what you should be doing, because you don't see yourself in action. The slightest alteration to the stance, grip or swing always feels uncomfortable to begin with, and doubts can soon eat away at your swing.

It's then you start drifting into old habits, simply because that's what comes naturally. Before long you're back to square one. But when the proof is there to see, it's much easier to set yourself back on the right lines.

SWING ON SCREEN
Every keen golfer has watched a tournament on television and admired the professional in action – picking up a tip or two on the way. With slow motion replays and comments from the experts, you almost feel you know certain golf swings as well as the player himself.

You can learn a great deal from studying your own swing – all you need is a video camera and one or two friends who are keen to improve their golf. The benefits apply to amateur golfers of all abilities – from the low handicap player to the raw beginner.

BEHIND THE LINES

Correct camera set-up is essential if you're to learn as much as possible from every shot. To start with have the person holding the camera positioned squarely to your right, looking down the line of your shot, as you take your stance.

The camera must be parallel to the target line. If it's fractionally off line it presents a confusing picture when you watch yourself in action later.

Your set-up determines the type of shot you hit. Often after you hit a bad shot you rack your brain trying to identify a chink in your swing.

Always look to your address position first – lay a club on the ground parallel to the target line to make sure your feet are aligned correctly. Check hips and shoulders are also on line. It would be a shame to hit a series of shots only to discover later you were aiming right or left.

On screen the first point to check is that your knees are nicely flexed at address. Bend from the waist and keep your back fairly straight – you should never be hunched over the ball.

Study the takeaway carefully – with the driver make sure you draw the club back low for 12in (30cm) slightly inside the ball-to-target line. Check the position of the club at the top of the backswing – it should point directly along the target line.

Notice how a poor backswing causes a fault later in the swing. If you take the club back outside the line, there's every chance it points left of target at the top. The reverse is true if you swing the club back too much inside the line. If you're in a poor position at the top you struggle to swing the club down on the correct path.

With the camera positioned to your right you have a perfect opportunity to study the path of the clubhead into impact – although you may need a slow motion replay to analyse this accurately. The main point to check is that the clubhead approaches the ball from inside the line.

CHECK ALIGNMENT, SWING PLANE AND PATH

CAMERA POINTS PARALLEL TO TARGET LINE